ISBN 978-9826717-I-9

The
The Magic of Color and the Secrets of Drawing
Everyone is an Artist

First in a Series of Basic 'How-To Art Books

A big 'Thank You' to all who
have attended my Demonstrations and
Workshops. I learned so much from you.

Fayrene Parrish

TABLE OF CONTENTS

Imagine - Visualize - Create!
......Finding Peace through the Joy of Art

Thank you for trying these ideas as you work with art. They are the basic principles and tools I've used over many years, and, have found to be the most helpful in creating a drawing or painting.

Not only have Imagination and Visualization helped me with many other issues unrelated to art, but they are the best and most rewarding tools for creating.

They have helped me relax and be more open to other levels of possibilities. In other words, imagination has been a fantastic tool. I'm sure you can understand how excited I was when I came across this quotation:

"Imagination is more important than knowledge. Knowledge is limited. Imagination encircles the world." ...Albert Einstein

'Visualization' - Imagine, or 'see a picture' on a screen inside your forehead,....in line with your nose, and about an inch above your eyes. This can give you a clear image of what you are dealing with. And then take a couple seconds and see it as clearly as possible Practice it. Practice it as many times per day as you can for several days. Soon you'll have this step down.....and just feel how those few moments of 'Visualization' have relaxed you.

'Creation' - Is carrying through with the picture or the idea. When you are involved with Creation, you become connected to 'all'. Quantum Science tells us that the energy of thought encircles the universe constantly, and that we all are one. We only need to be open to the ideas that flow via the energy flowing around and through us, to have access to answers.

Recent Medical Science has proven how healthy it is to play with art, and to be creative. It lowers your blood pressure, and relaxes one both physically and mentally.

So, have fun and may you find Peace through the Joy of Art.

MATERIALS NEEDED FOR DRAWING

(Available at local Art Supply Stores, and On-line under 'Art Supplies'). The * indicates tools needed to work with his introductory book. All will be needed as you continue drawing and coloring.)

BLACK CHARCOAL STICKS

WHITE CHALK

MALLEABLE GUM TYPE ERASERS, and/or ERASER PENCILS *

#2 LEAD and #4 LEAD DRAWING PENCILS - Wooden, that can be * sharpened

PEN HOLDERS (with Multiple pen shapes and types) & INK (black and/or colored)

RUBBING STICK to blend charcoal and Pastel colors

LEAD PENCILS (MULTI-COLORED TOO, for coloring *

PASTELS OR OIL PASTELS sticks - multi-colored

A SMALL, PORTABLE PENCIL SHARPENER *

PAPERS: Drawing paper for: CHARCOAL; PENCILS & PENS

A CLOTH or PAPER TOWELS to wipe your hands

A SMALL WATER HOLDER (PLASTIC CUP) & A BOTTLE OF WATER

PAPERS (8-1/2 x 10"): *Drawing paper* for: CHARCOAL; PENCILS & PENS *
     ***Gessoed watercolor paper* for: Pastels or Oil pastels**

NOTE: If you are a beginner and wish to use watercolor,I would suggest using a #8 brush, watercolor paper and *'Finger Paints'*. Finger Paints are liquid, and very easy to use.....just blend with a little water to dilute.

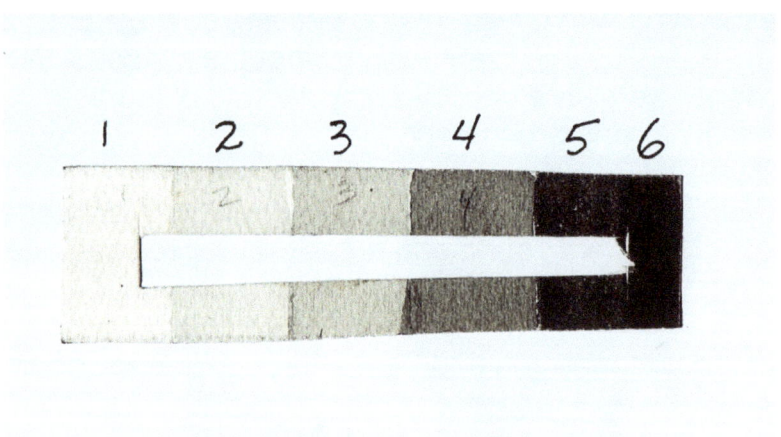

AN 'EASY TO MAKE' VALUE FINDER

If you print out several copies of the value finder, and put them next to your Primary and Secondary colors as you begin coloring or painting, it will make it lot easier to get familiar with values......and will give you values to use to create the shaping of objects you are creating.

Another favorite Value Finders, is a made by Value Comp at artworksessentials.com   .....it is a see-through, red cellophane, with the values up to 10. Bought it awhile back, so don't know if its still available. If not available, some artists just use a piece of **red**, 'see-through', fairly stiff *cellophane* or *plastic.*   It's a tool a lot of photographers use too.

So, let's get started.......

LET'S TRY THESE SHAPES

Easily draw any line, shape or space using the following 'Connect the Dots' trick. First the CIRCLE. using your pencil, MARK a TOP DOT and a BOTTOM DOT, using a 'clock face' as your guide. Put the top dot at 12:00; the bottom dot at 6:00 on the clock...THEN the SECONDARY DOTS - 3:00 &9:00. Add more dots - as many as you like, in between these...Then 'Connect the Dots' with your pencil ...and you have a Circle!

.

The spaces between all the dots should be carefully placed to create the

.   .

shape you are ultimately reaching. Use as many dots as feel comfortable.

.

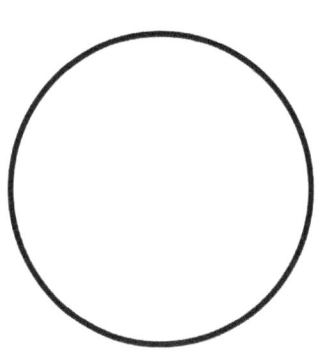

Any shape can be created with this 'trick'.   So, let's try the next page and try some other shapes.

Put dots in between these dots, and then connect them with a line….to create a **wave-like, curved** line.

How about a
Square?

Works for an
Oblong
(use red dots) too.

And, now a
Triangle

By practicing the drawing of these few shapes, and then combining shapes as needed, you **can draw** just about anything. (*Wish I'd known this trick when I started drawing*).

PRIMARY
COLORS

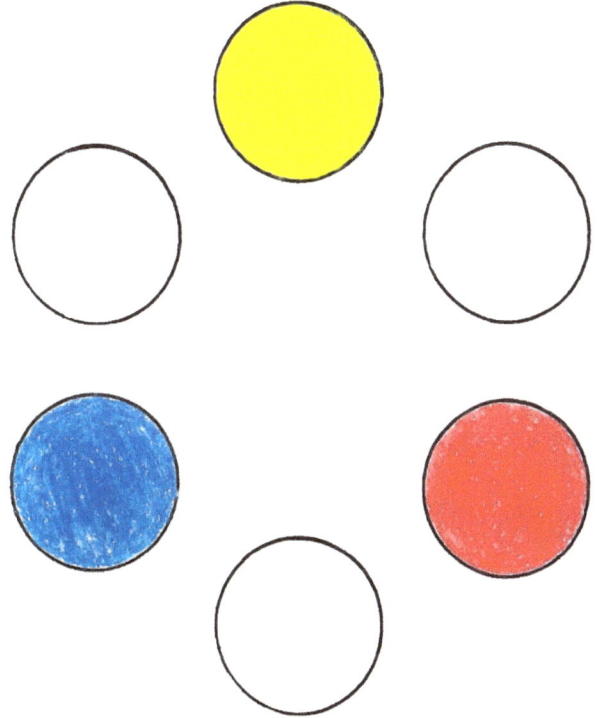

...You can see them too.....The Primary Colors RED, **YELLOW** and **BLUE**. Isn't **YELLOW** the color of the *SUN* so bright, and **BLUE** the color of *WATER*. Now-- mix **YELLOW** and **BLUE**... and you get *GREEN*, the color of *GROWTH* we've all seen. ...*Red* represents the *LOVE* we all know.....so mix RED, YELLOW and BLUE, and you get BROWN, the color of *MOTHER EARTH*, from whence all doth grow...3 of the most important *ELEMENTS* indeed, from which we all evolved, grow, glow and spread a seed.

SECONDARY COLORS

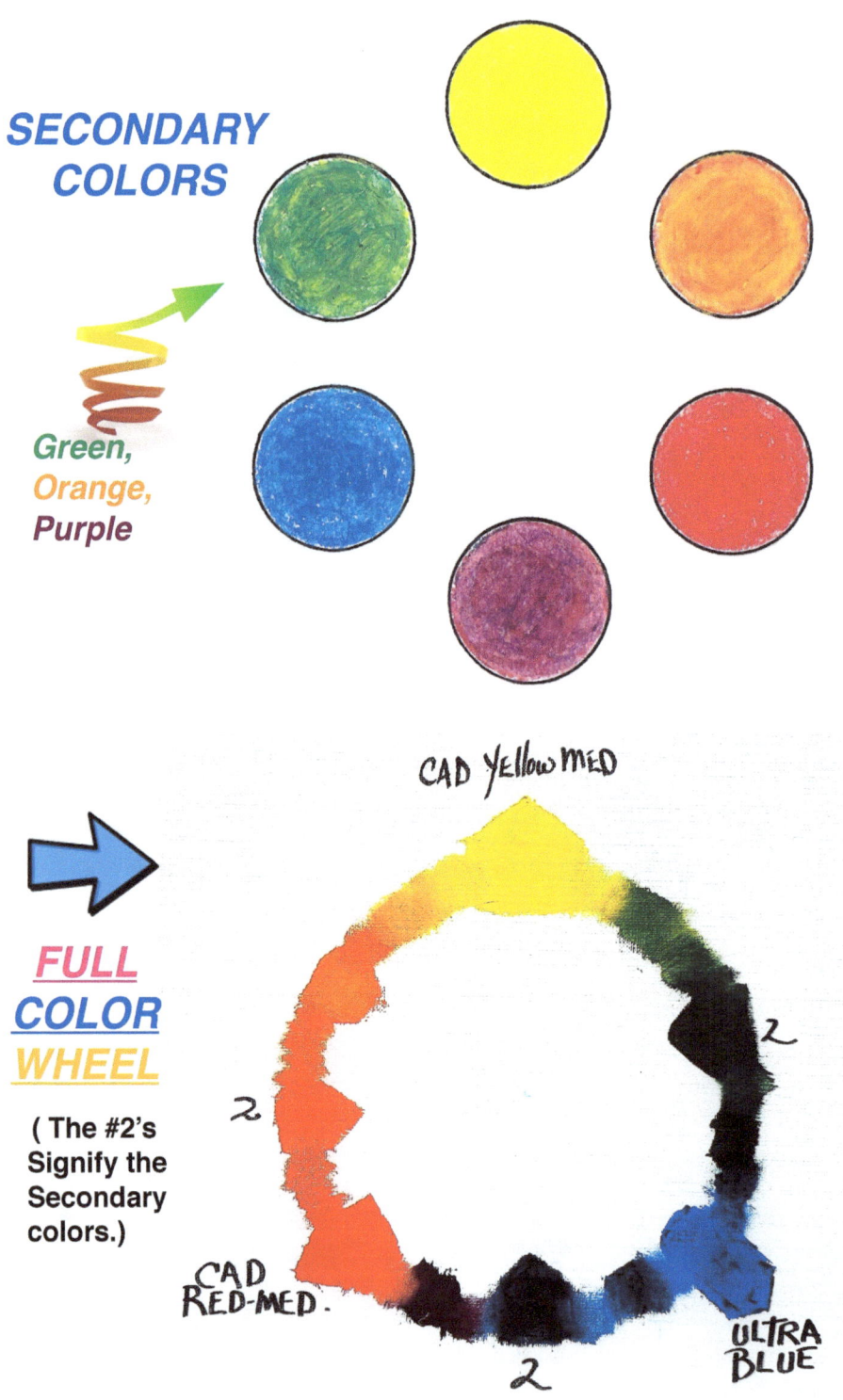

Green,
Orange,
Purple

CAD YELLOW MED

FULL COLOR WHEEL

(The #2's Signify the Secondary colors.)

2

2

CAD RED-MED.

2

ULTRA BLUE

By using the 'Primary Colors' you create the Secondary Colors… Green, Yellow & Orange. Blend them together & you have a full color wheel. Keep going, and you can create every color in the world! That's what I call…."The Magic of Color".

Use dots to 'shape' the shadow. Connect the dots and begin. As you practice this, you will begin to see more and more 'light and dark' in the object & its shadow. Follow what you see and use your instincts.

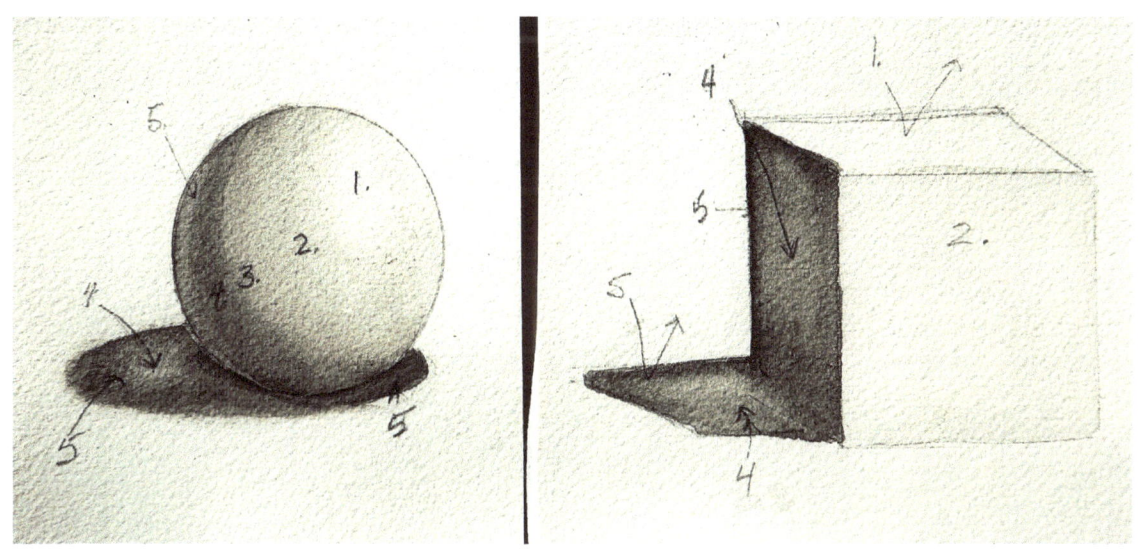

For coloring your shapes, and a more realistic shadow-look, **use Ultramarine Blue and Burnt Sienna in** watercolor, acrylics or any type of pastels, or color pencils And, you can be experimental, and use any color ......Be Abstract!

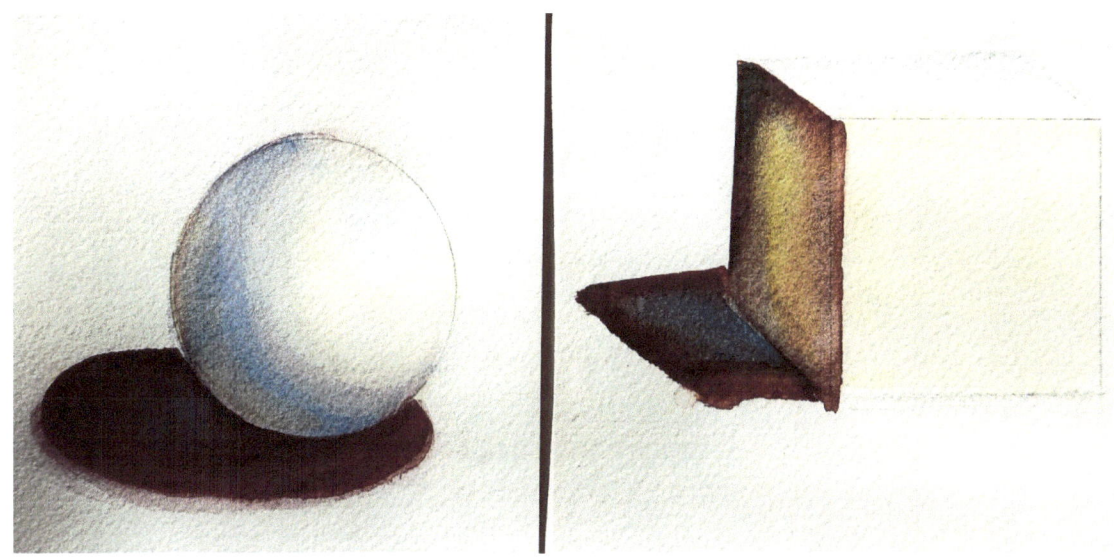

TO HELP OPEN THE DOOR TO
"IMAGINE....VISUALIZE....AND CREATE!"

Each day, for a month (to get in the habit) sit down in a comfortable, quiet place with no distractions. Turn off all audio equipment, and especially your cell phone. It's best to do this as soon as you can in the morning, before you start an art project or the days' activities. Then write in your diary:

1. Your impressions of :
   Sound
   Smells
   Music
   Nature Sounds - rain, creek running, bird calls, animal noises

By this I mean, how they make you feel, what you see in your minds eye, ('Visualization'), and what memories might be invoked. Can you apply colors, weather atmospheres or moods for a drawing or painting to these? What do they inspire?

2. How do you feel about what you painted yesterday?
   Would you like to change or add something to bring it more to what you wanted it to say?
   What do you plan to paint today?
   What skill do you wish to focus on?

3. Make a outline of your painting project by answering the questions we have already gone over, and perhaps others.

   A value study
   The mood; the atmosphere; the style
   And, keep in mind the skill you are focusing on.

So-o.....Relax, enjoy and have fun. Remember there ARE *NO* MISTAKES in art. Create your *own* visual expressions.
Have fun......find peace, and create joy.
If you have any questions, you can reach me at:

My website.

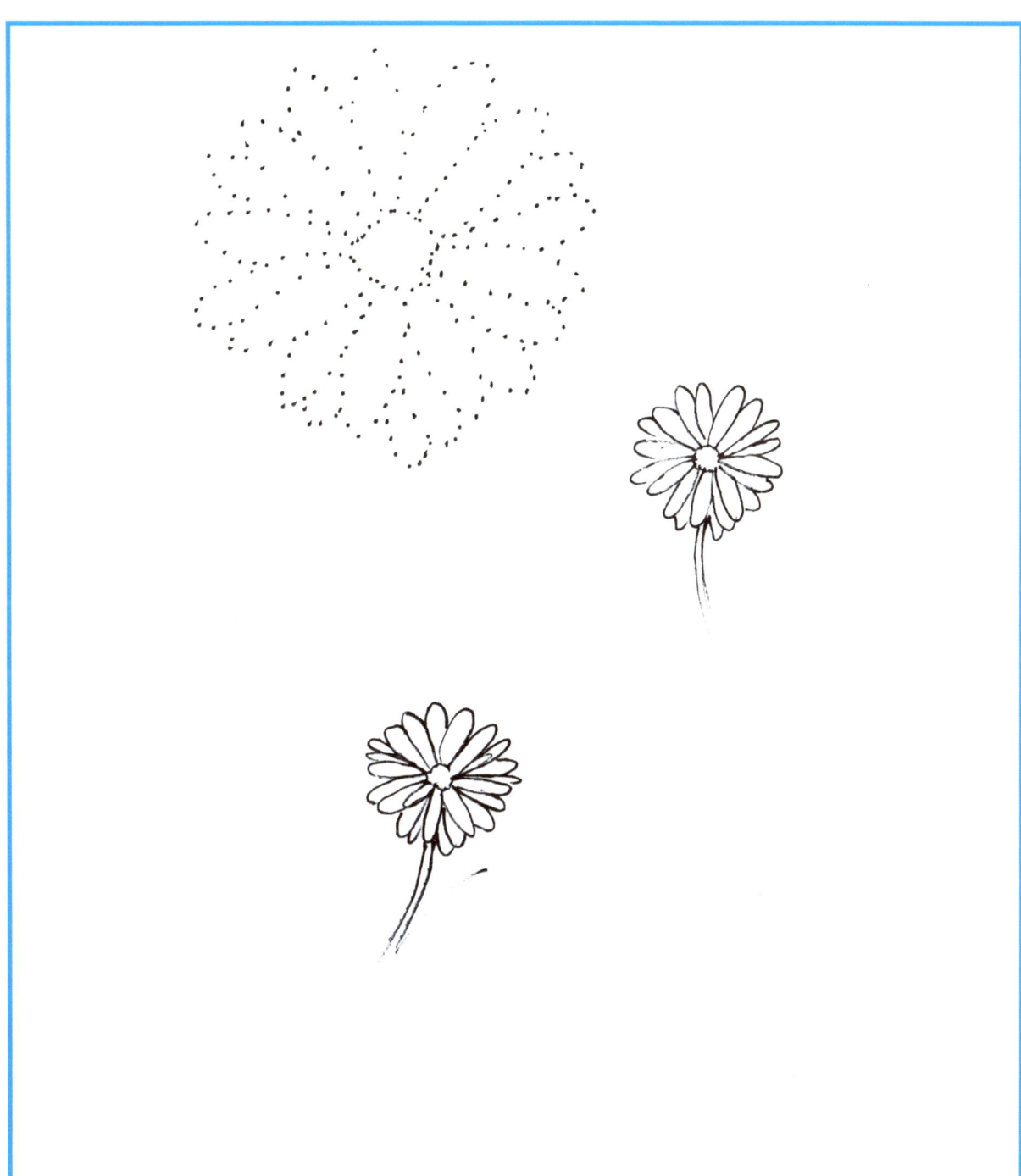

9

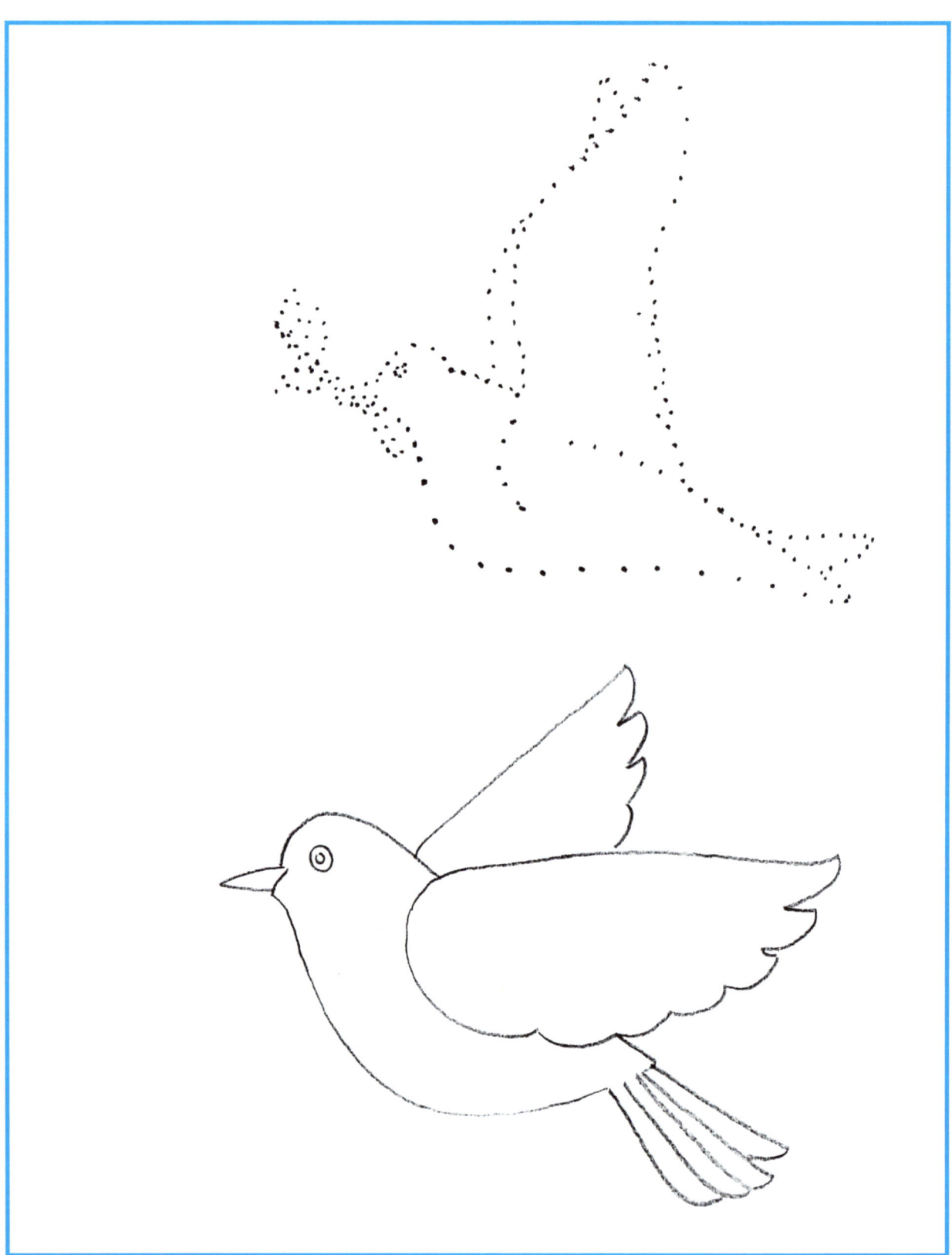

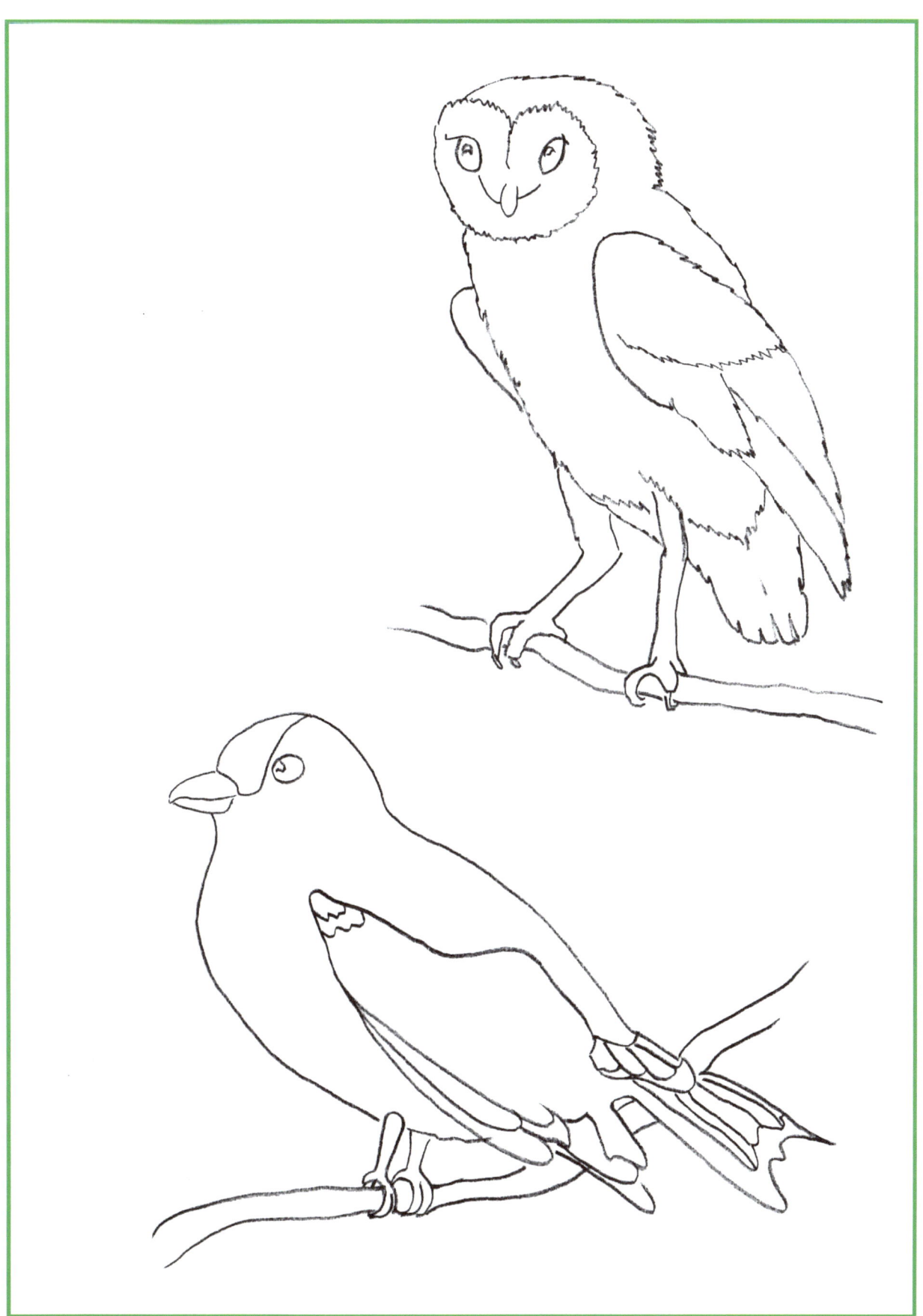

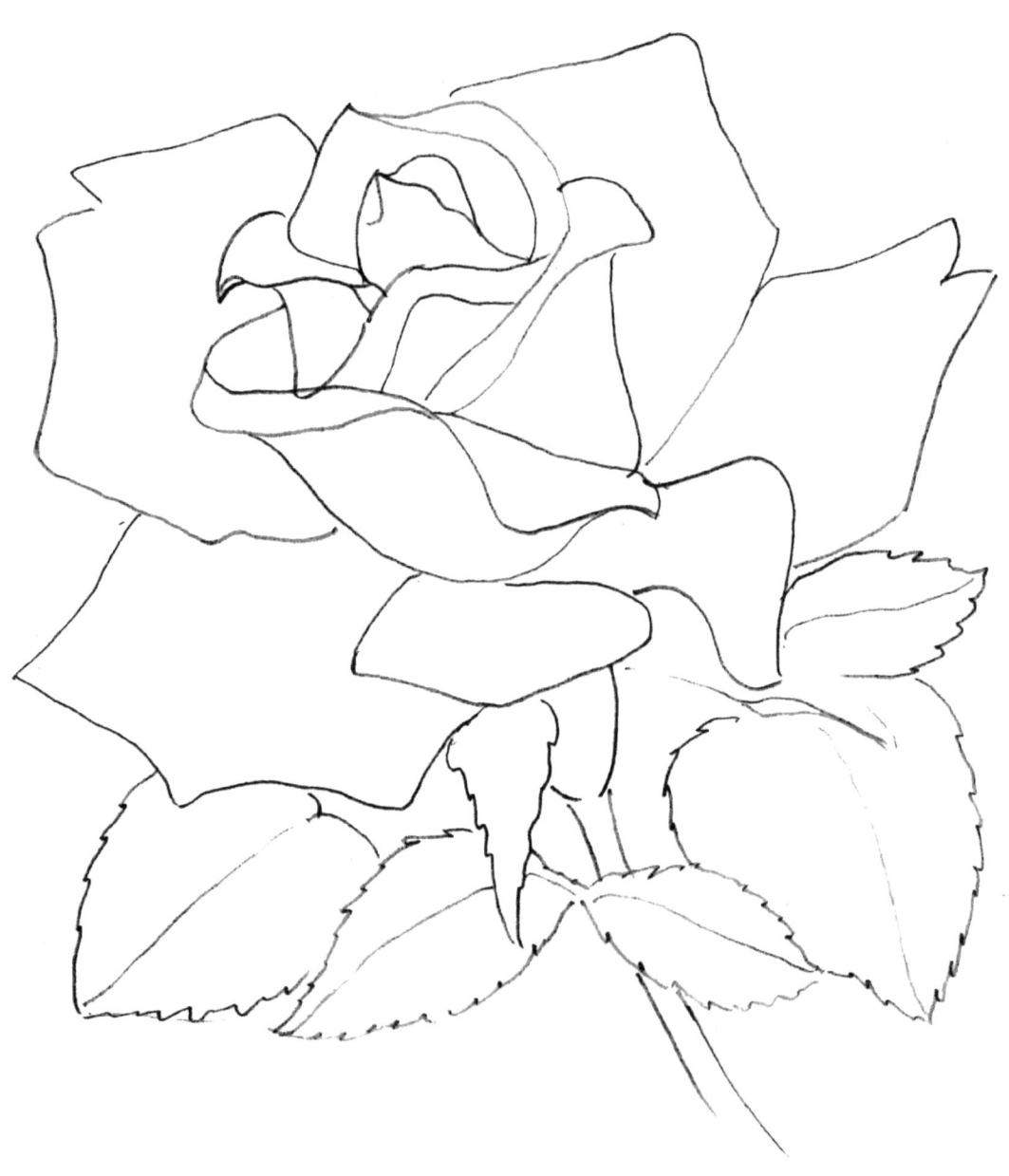

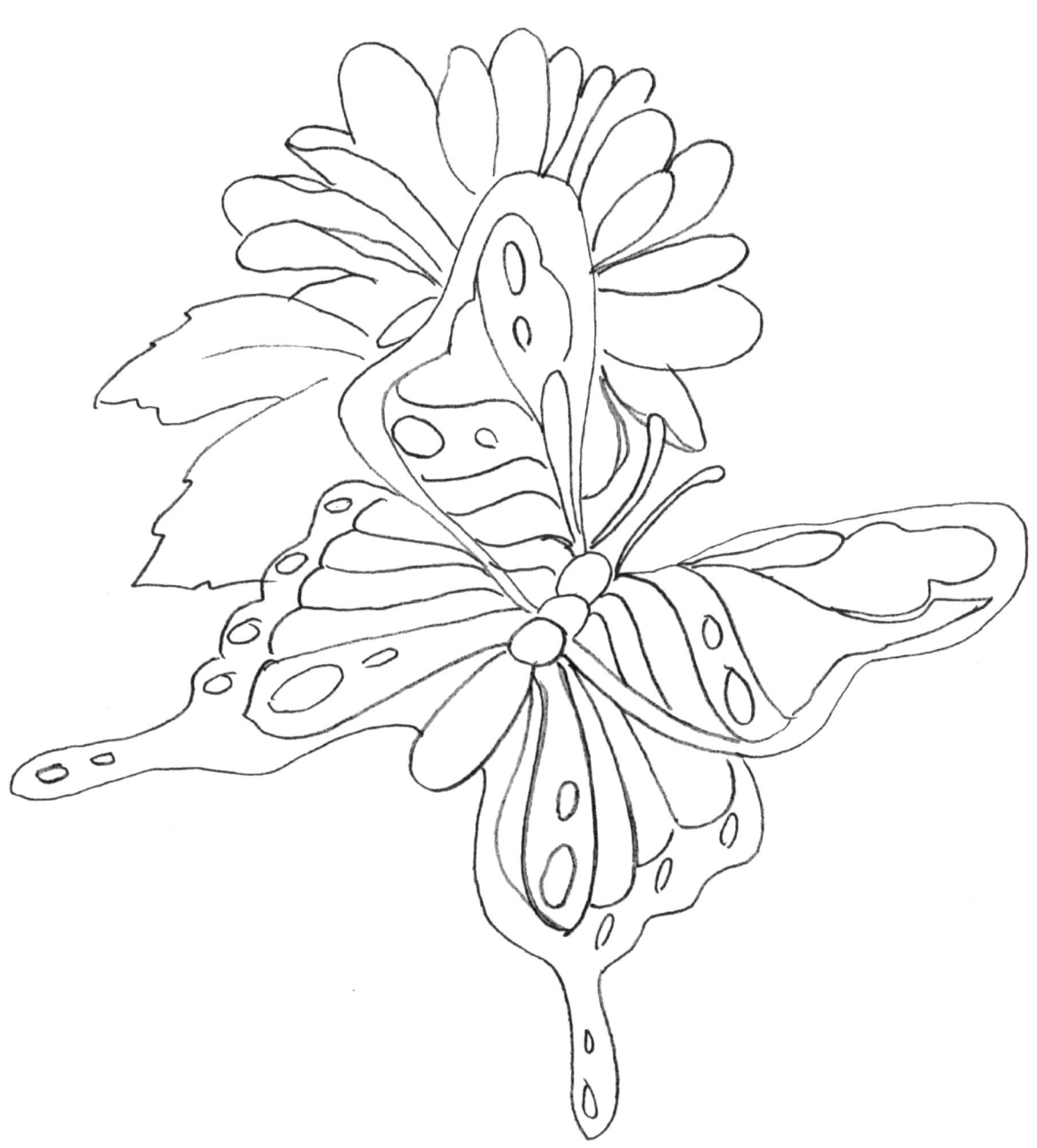

Now that you've worked with 'nature' a bit, how about a few subjects you might want to color and use as a 'greeting card'…or send with a scanned note via e-mail?

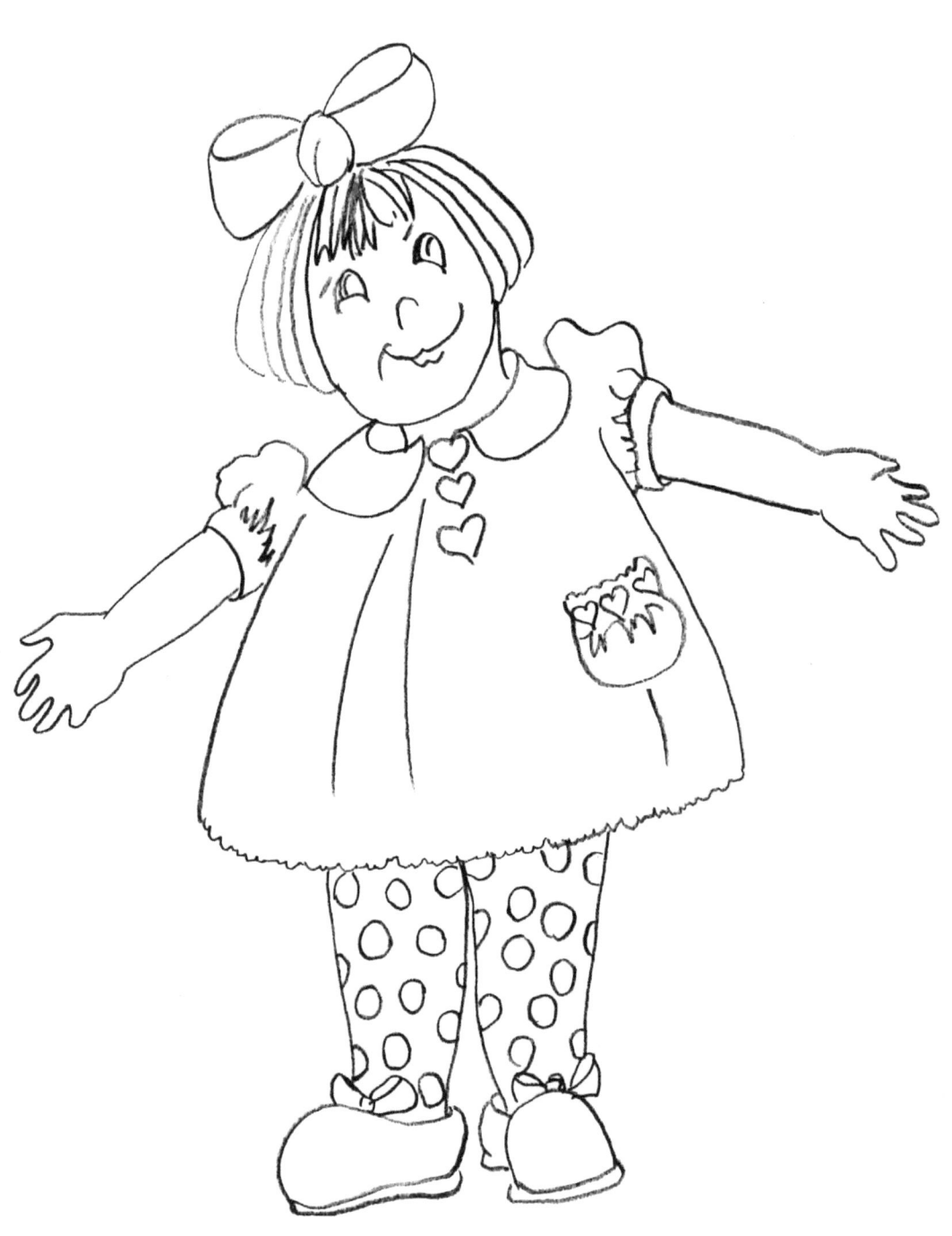

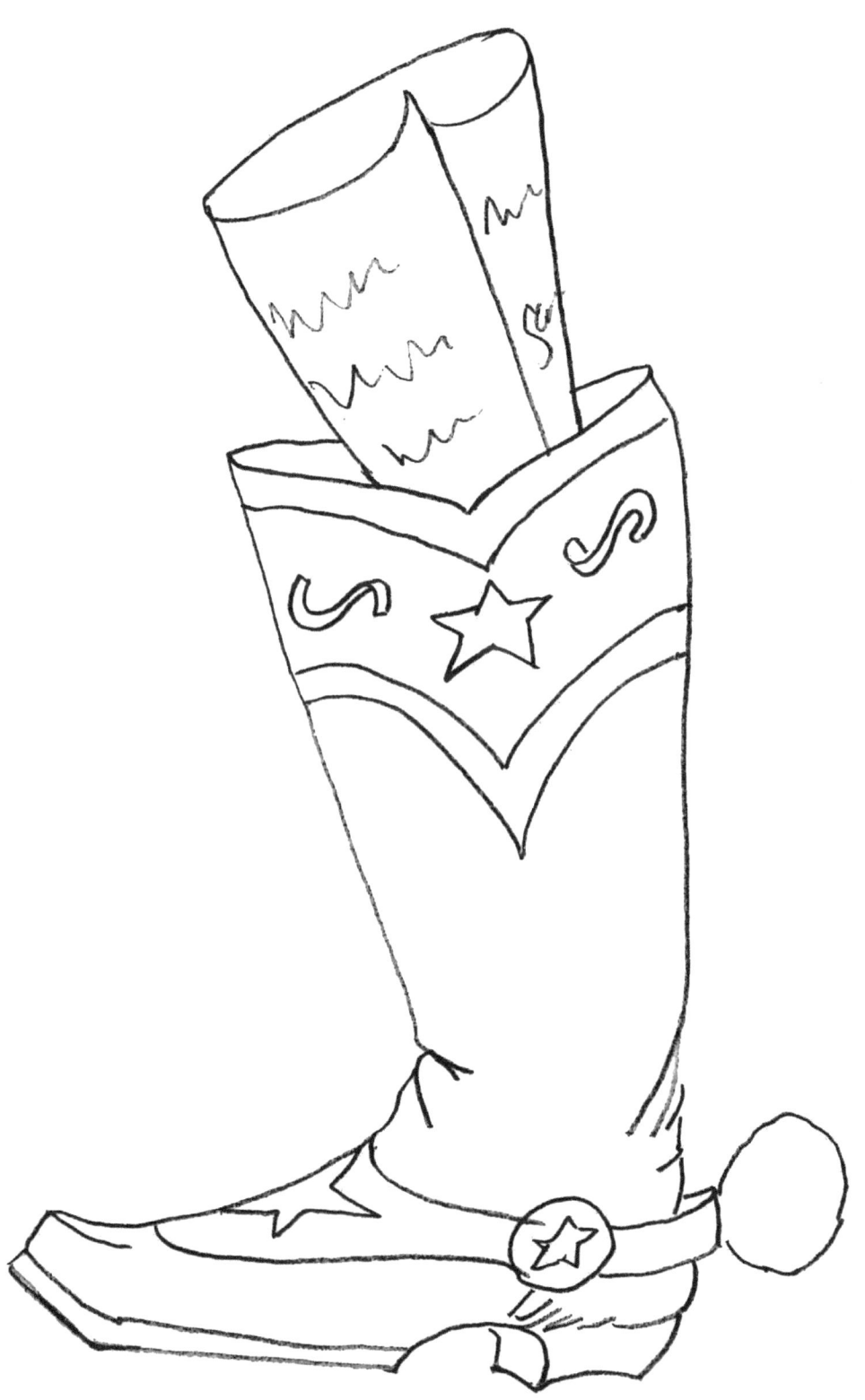

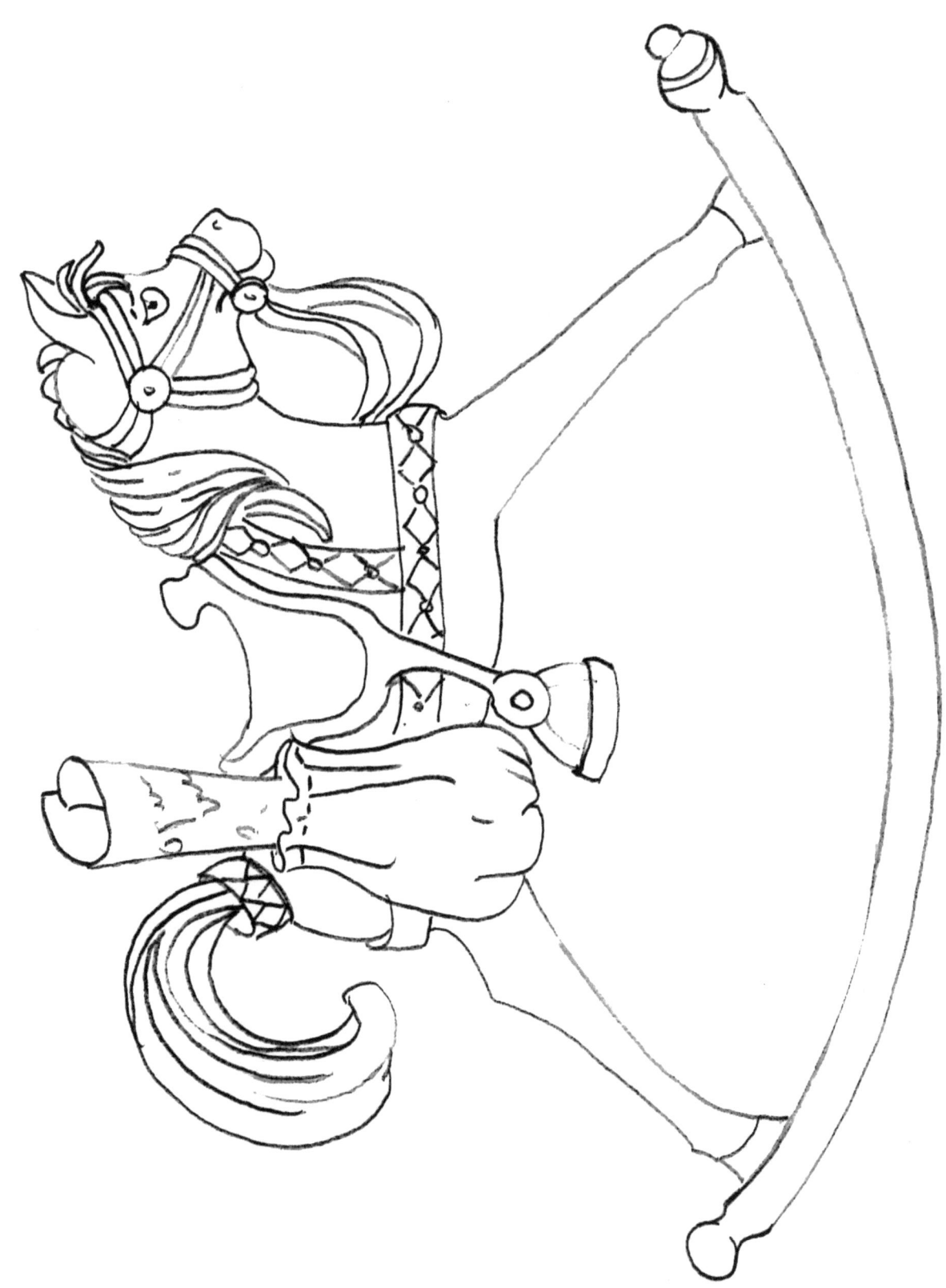

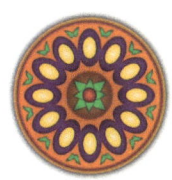

LET'S TRY CREATING SOME MANDALAS

Mandalas are a beautiful form of art that allows one to draw and color without extensive drawing or art lessons. Of course the most beautiful ones we've all seen have been created by those who have practiced this form for many years.

So, now that you know the 'Secrets of Line', and the Magic of Color', you can easily create your own Mandalas. It's a wonderful path to relaxation, and a great form of contemplative meditation.

Following are some Basic Foundations to start building your own Mandalas .... using the 'tricks' of creating shapes we've just gone through. Just use dots to add shapes to them, connect them with line, then use the 'Magic' you've been working with to color them.

The shapes you choose to add will be ones that express your feelings and thoughts. The colors chosen will add depth to those feelings and thoughts.

Before creating a Mandala, try sitting in a quite space...relaxing your body - three deep yoga-type breaths really help, and then empty your mind of all stress, anxiety and outside thoughts. Just let them *go*. Meditate on emptiness. Visualize a clear, sky-blue, empty space. Try taking a walk, sitting outside and watching Nature at work...watching the birds and butterflies, the breeze blowing leafs, nature sounds around you.

If an emotional uplift is needed, sometimes listening to hand clappin', foot stompin' music helps. Even getting up, moving to the rhythm, works too.*

Many more Mandala shapes are available 'on-line'. Just use your browser and search: 'Free clip art for Mandalas'.

*Here's some YouTube music you can click thru to, on your computer...they help raise spirits and create Joy. I use some of these a lot, not only for my morning exercises but to start my art Demos and Workshops.

type in: www.Youtube.com
       Once there,....... in the top empty slot, type in
           Irish Rovers singing "Green Alligators" , and
              "The Lord of The Dance"
           Frank French "Womba Momba"
           "Voices of Spring Waltz" - Johann Strauss Jr.
           The Beach Boys, "Surfin' the USA"

Some Basic Shapes for Creating Your Own Mandalas

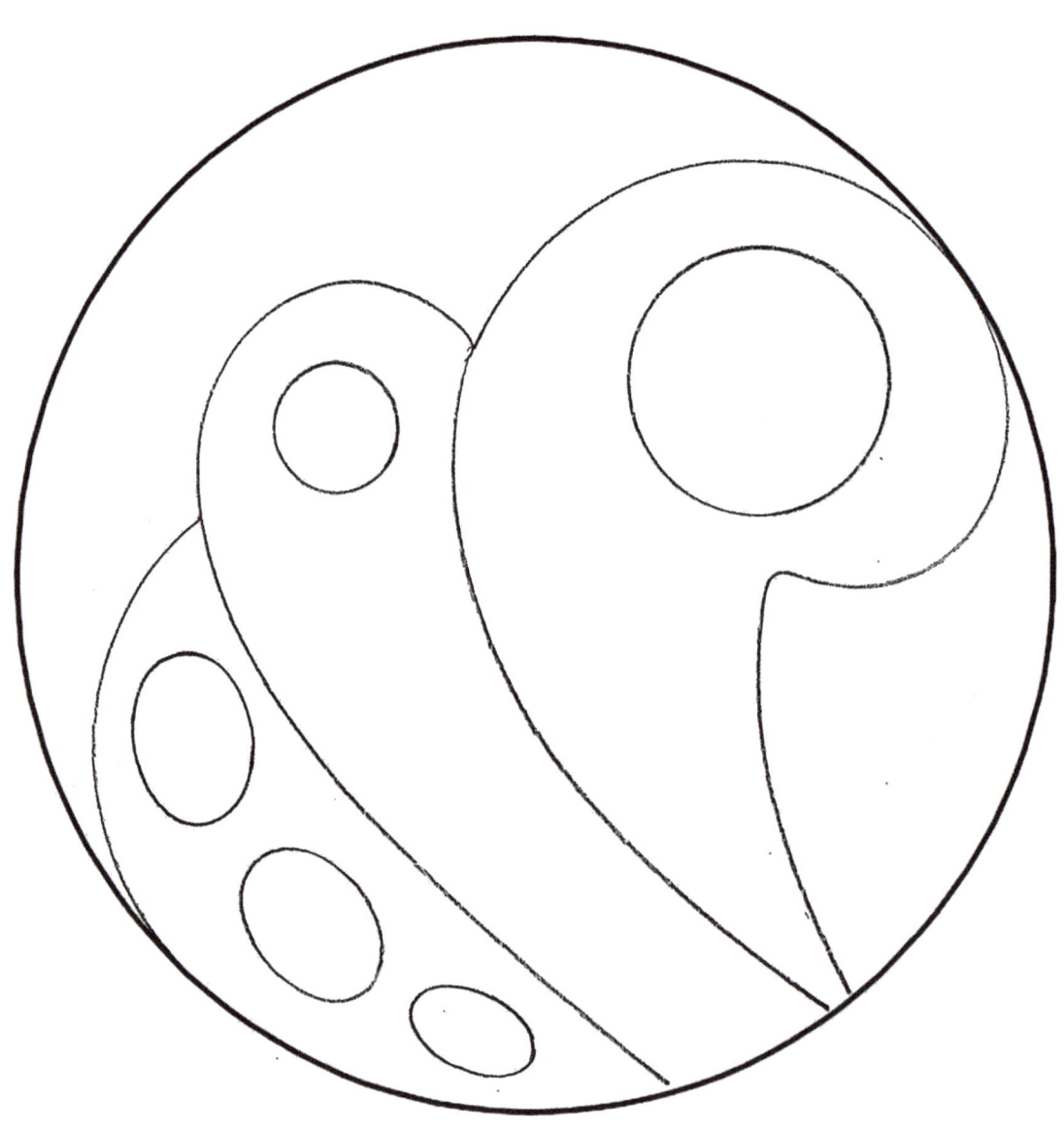

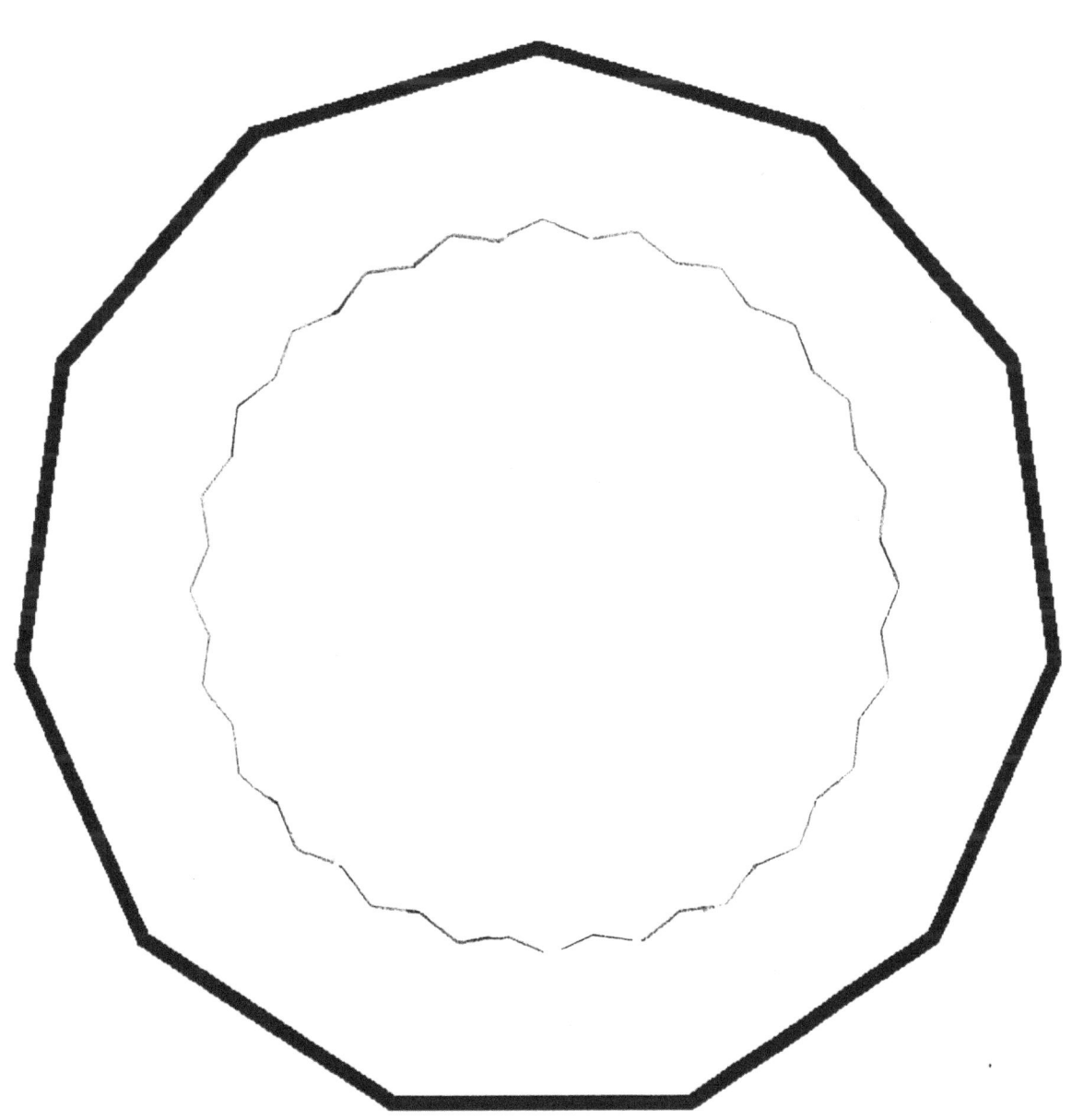

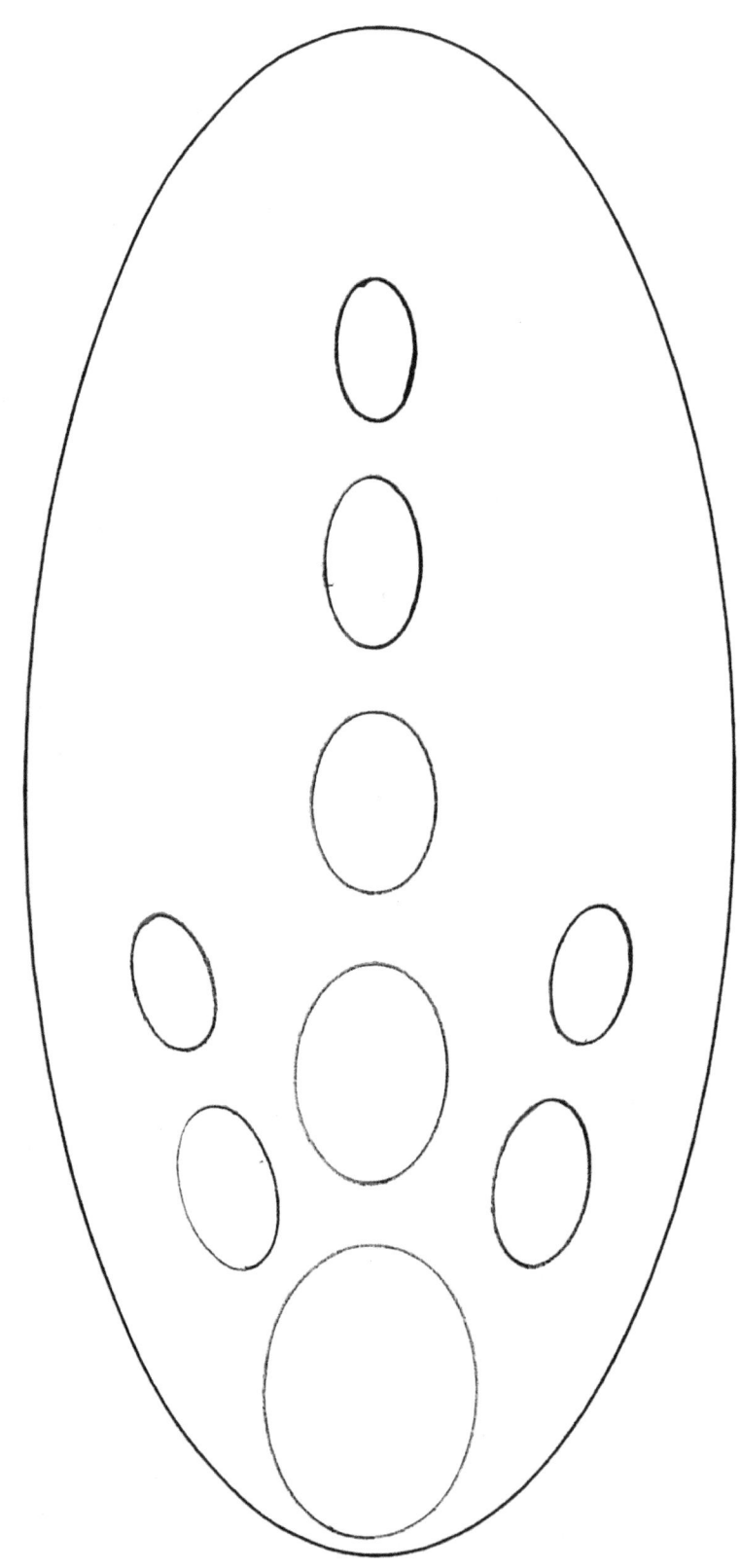

Quotations also Inspire Mandalas

"The more I think about it, the more I realize there is nothing more artistic than to love others."

Vincent Van Gogh

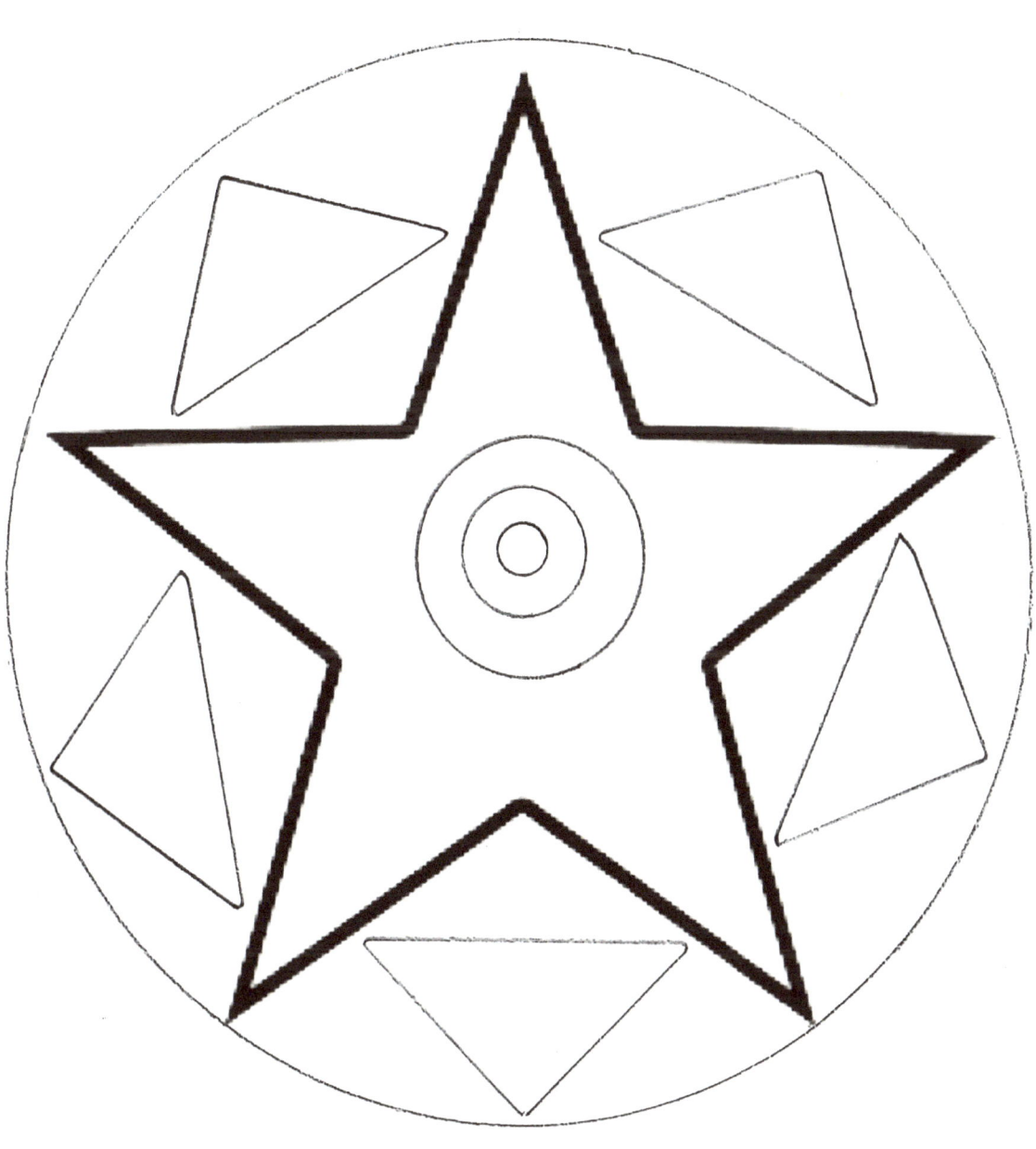

Some Quotes to Ponder.....

I try to apply colors like words that shape poems, like notes that shape music. .... *Joan Miro*

****

"Imagination is more important than knowledge. Knowledge is limited. Imagination encircles the world".......*Albert Einstein*

****

"If you hear a voice within you say 'you cannot paint,' then by all means paint ant that voice will be silenced.

.........*Vincent Van Gogh*

****

"First, one seeks to become an artist by training the hand. Then one finds it is the eye that needs improving. Later one learns it is the mind that wants developing, only to find that the ultimate quest of the artist is in the spirit". *Larry Brullo*

******

"When you are 'open', the unconscious flowering of the blossom within begins".

"Art Makes Thought Visible"....*Fayrene Parrish*

****

"There are only two mistakes one can make along the road to truth; not going all the way, and not starting."........................*Buddha*

Truly hope this basic intro to drawing and coloring has inspired you to continue creating and expressing yourself through art. If not right away, you will over time, find that Art really does create relaxation, and that all stress and anxiety slip away while you focus on your art creation.

If you have any questions, or would like a critique, you can contact me on my website.

****

Thanks again, for trying these 'secrets' and 'magic tricks' learned over time. And, ...more will be coming soon.

Also, if you're a Home Schooler, or Pre-Schooler, or need some fun for Children's Vacations, my Children's 'Shipmates Learning Adventures' (all in Coloring Book format) are going up on line too. They travel the world in search of Adventure and explorations of various Environments.....as well as multiple Art Lessons. There are 4 lead characters that make up the crew aboard the 'Good Ship Scooter'......Capt. Bear, Admiral Bird, Huff'n Puffin, and Pancho The Salty Sea Dog.

So, (because I, too have been a sailor for most of my adult life) - *"May you have fair winds and smooth seas"*.

Fayrene

FAYRENE PARRISH
www.fayreneparrish.com

A native of California, she began her artistic career as an actress, and segued into the fine art world as a sculptor, printmaker and painter. Her 'work' is in collections of major corporations, hotels, private collections and offices including the United States Government, as well as galleries in the United States, Europe and Australia..

Involvement with the community has included the establishment of Art Programs and Art Scholarships for both Adults and Children, Art Exhibitions and Galleries. She organized and founded The Malibu Art Colony, The Sculpture Association in San Luis Obispo and art programs during her stay in the Northwest. Most recently she founded the California Annual Sculpture in Cambria, and "Art From The Heart"for Retirement communities....view on YouTube: https://www.youtube.com/watch?v=QlO3N36wzDE

Fayrene is a Retired member of the California Art Club, the Oil Painters of America, San Louis Obispo Painters for The Environment, the Ojai Studio Artists and Plein Air Painters of America; current member of Ojai Community Art Center, and has been invited to teach workshops in Hawaii, Italy   and France as well as throughout the Western States.

Her work has been shown in in the Museum of Natural History, Los Angeles; America House in New York, Gold Medal Shows for the California Art Club. and the Museum of Art in Skagit County, Washington.

Artist Statement

"I've been fortunate to have worked in many media, printmaking (as an etcher), watercolor and now back to my first loves - sculpture and oils.

Sculpture *has always been a wonderful challenge whether in stone, clay or bronze. I might have a specific goal in mind when I begin, but the medium always joins in my silent conversation so that a similar but different piece results.*

Plein air painting *is just the opposite. It's relaxing - time is suspended when outside with canvas and easel. Painting outdoors is one of the joys of being an artist. After I've settled down and have been painting for awhile, the birds and creatures return and fill the air with their sounds. Some of my most precious memories have been provided by critters stumbling upon me while I'm painting or sketching"*

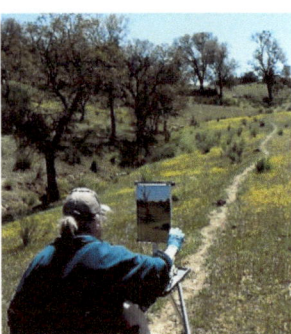

Carrizo Plain, California

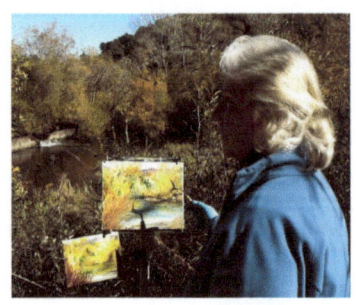

San Louis Creek,San Louis Obispo, Ca.

www.ingramcontent.com/pod-product-compliance
Lightning Source LLC
Chambersburg PA
CBHW050427180526
45159CB00005B/2438